No More Bad-Hair Days

A Woman's Journey

through Cancer,

Chemotherapy

and Coping

Susan Sturges Hyde

LONGSTREET PRESS
Atlanta, Georgia

Published by LONGSTREET PRESS, INC.,
a subsidiary of Cox Newspapers,
a subsidiary of Cox Industries, Inc.
2140 Newmarket Parkway
Suite 122
Marietta, Georgia 30067

Printed in the United States of America

1st printing, 1997

Library of Congress Card Catalog Number: 96-79804

ISBN: 1-56352-412-0

Jacket design by Tonya Beach
Book design by Jill Dible

*I*n loving memory of my mother, Mary Torode Hieatt, and my grandmothers, Pauline Roberts Torode and Ruth Evans Sturges, who walked this road before me. Their dignity — in every circumstance — instructed me in grace and strength.

*E*ach year in the United States, more than half a million women are diagnosed with cancer. In 1996, I was one of those women.

Three doctors concurred that I had advanced ovarian cancer. I was 53, divorced, and a single mother with three children, but at the moment of diagnosis, I felt completely alone.

I was referred to a fourth doctor, Matthew Burrell, an Atlanta oncologist specializing in female cancers. Dr. Burrell has a fine reputation and is a caring and concerned physician. He is also my friend.

After my examination, we talked. Matt agreed with the original diagnosis but did not think the cancer had spread to my lungs or lymph nodes. (This turned out to be correct.)

He also felt that because I was a non-smoker, a semi-vegetarian, exercised moderately, and practiced yoga, my healthy lifestyle would aid in my overcoming cancer. But it was Matt's parting words that intrigued me the most: "Susan, because of your attitude and the zest and joy you express in living, I believe that together we can cure you."

Matt had his part to do with surgery and chemotherapy. I had my part to do with attitude. (This is when being an incurable optimist is an advantage!)

At this time, I have undergone extensive surgery and six months of chemotherapy. Although I did not reach remission, I chose to forego additional chemotherapy. Enough is enough. I am happily exploring alternative methods of healing. I feel wonderful and am certain that I will be completely well again.

My family, my friends, my physician and his staff, and the superb staff at Saint Joseph's Hospital in Atlanta, have loved, encouraged, and supported me throughout the various stages of my illness. Thousands of prayers have been sent up, and God has blessed me with a spirit of indomitability. My love of life continues to grow and expand in new directions.

I wanted to write about my situation and my experiences so that other women could be better prepared for fighting their own battles. This is a time when you need all the help you can get.

Each year in the United States more that 15,000 women die of ovarian cancer. I don't intend to be a victim of cancer and neither should you.

*T*here are few women who, when faced with the certainty of losing their hair, can bravely proclaim that at least for a while they won't have any more bad-hair days. My friend Susan Sturges Hyde is one of those people.

This book is Susan's way of doing what she's always done — spread humor, insight, and good practical advice to all those around. This time the subject is cancer. And this time, we're listening more closely than ever.

No More Bad-Hair Days was conceived as a way to pass the time, to write down funny thoughts, to express emotion, and to share with others. It became a passion and a reason for living. Now it is a gift to fellow travelers. Please enjoy this book, as it was lovingly and painstakingly handwritten over several months of diagnosis, surgery, treatment, and healing. It was written for every woman in the world who has endured the same and for those who love her.

— MELISSA LIBBY

No More Bad-Hair Days

Cancer is not for sissies.

∞∞∞

It's best not to ask, why me? No one really
knows the answer to that question, and you
can drive yourself crazy trying to figure it out.

∞∞∞

It is okay to cry when your hair falls out,
but it's more fun to imagine what it will
look like when it grows back in.

1

As an adult, there is still a lot of comfort to
be found in the simple childhood prayer,
"Now I lay me down to sleep . . ."

∞∞∞

Even your best friends don't love you
as much as your dog does.

∞∞∞

The longer you are undergoing
chemotherapy, the wearier you get.
If you understand this at the beginning
of your treatment, you won't be so
discouraged toward the end.

No More Bad-Hair Days

The twenty-third Psalm is still the best.

∞∞∞

When you are told that your hair is
going to fall out, cut it *short*. It is less
traumatic to lose short hair than long hair.

∞∞∞

People are always delighted
when their thoughtfulness is acknowledged
with a thank-you note.

∞∞∞

A sick adult should never have to share
a telephone with two teenagers.

Nothing brings more hope than
fall bulbs bursting into spring flowers.

∞∞∞∞

Laughter really is the best medicine.

∞∞∞∞

No one can predict how even the best of
friends will react in a crisis.

∞∞∞∞

Hats are great, but hair is better.

A plump teddy bear is a wonderful get-well
gift as well as a great sleeping buddy.
Teddy bears don't snore or hog the bed covers.

∞∞∞

Having temporarily given up both sex and
wine, I can tell you that I miss wine more.

∞∞∞

There truly is something positive
about the power of positive thinking.

No More Bad-Hair Days

Hospital food is hazardous to your health.

∞∞∞

Don't be embarrassed to ask for help.

∞∞∞

There is no such thing as receiving too many
flowers when you are in the hospital.

∞∞∞

Books truly are the gifts that keep on giving.

No More Bad-Hair Days

The cost of health care in America
is unaffordable — even for the rich.

∞∞∞∞

Eight glasses of water a day —
even when it is bottled and has a designer
label — still seems like a lot.

∞∞∞∞

A picnic on your bed, shared with a dear
friend, is just as good as a trip to the park.

A plastic bottle of soapy bubbles with a
little magic wand kept next to your bed
can provide you with many moments of joy.

∞∞

Self-help books really can help.

∞∞

There is absolutely nothing wrong with
staying in bed and resting all day
if that is what you want to do.

Your dog knows intuitively when you are
sick and gives you comfort. Your cat
couldn't care less.

∞∞∞

The more cheerful you act,
the more cheerful you feel.

∞∞∞

Major surgery is so important
that it should be promoted to General.

No More Bad-Hair Days

Living with cancer is like living with an
uninvited, unwanted house guest.
Eventually, both will be gone.

∞∞∞

Before surgery, treat yourself to a pedicure.
You'll spend a lot of time in bed staring at
your feet, so they might as well look pretty.

∞∞∞

Don't let your feelings be hurt when you
don't hear from your friends everyday. They
are still as busy as you used to be.

No More Bad-Hair Days

No matter how much weight you lose
to cancer and chemotherapy, you can still
have chubby thighs.

∞∞∞

Good therapy is a walk through a garden
in full bloom. Even better is picking
a bouquet to take home.

∞∞∞

Oncologists are like ship captains. Choose
yours wisely as he will be guiding you through
a lot of rough seas and choppy waters.

No matter how ill you are, if you love to
dance, it's impossible not to "tap your toes"
when you hear a good tune on the radio.

∞∞∞

Buy yourself an orchid plant. They are low
maintenance, produce exquisite flowers, and
their blooms can last for months.

∞∞∞

When you go for chemotherapy or
blood work, take a sweater. Hospitals are like
iceboxes, and cancer makes you cold.

No matter how many years you've dieted
and maintained great eating habits,
when your doctor advises you to gain weight,
you'll grab for desserts first!

∞∞∞

Even the worst days can contain some
magical moments. Look for them.

∞∞∞

It is perfectly all right to tell the truth when
someone asks you how you're feeling.
Remember, no one is "fine" all of the time.

No More Bad-Hair Days

There are times when wearing a wig is about
as comfortable as trying to wear a cat.

ꝏꝏ

This, too, shall pass.

ꝏꝏ

Chemotherapy makes you feel like a cross
between a guinea pig and a pin cushion.

No More Bad-Hair Days

It is good to discuss your cancer and its treatment with your friends. They want to understand so that they can help.

∞∞∞

When your nurse hangs up the "no visitors" sign and has your bedside phone turned off, don't argue. You need the rest.

∞∞∞

When your hair is gone, just think of the money you'll save on shampoo!

No More Bad-Hair Days

Each day of your illness brings
a new learning experience.

∞∞∞

If you focus on getting well rather than on
being sick, the days fly by faster.

∞∞∞

Try to book the first appointment in the
morning with your doctor. Once you're
finished, you have an early start on an
enjoyable day. And you're already dressed!

Illness will bring old friends back
into your life. Welcome them and put aside
the reasons they were gone.

∞∞∞

Prayers are like good conversations. The more
you put into them, the easier they flow.

∞∞∞

Having cancer is like going to college.
It begins as an interesting learning
experience, but not too long into it,
you can't wait to graduate.

No More Bad-Hair Days

It is perfectly all right to skip your bath.
After all, how dirty can you get in bed, alone?

⚬⚬⚬⚬⚬

Don't fret about the things you can't do now.
Focus on what you can do. Life will return to
its usual hustle-bustle soon enough.

⚬⚬⚬⚬⚬

Nurses are like mothers. They know best.

While you are in the hospital, if your daughter wrecks your car, just remember that right now you can't drive anyway.

∞∞∞

The older I get, the more I realize that it takes less and less to make me happy.

∞∞∞

No matter how beautiful the scarf, no matter how I try to tie it, when I get it on my head, it still looks like a babushka.

I go to bed exhausted and I wake up tired, but I am always really, really happy to wake up!

∞∞∞

Never again will I criticize a man who tries to hide his bald spot by letting his hair grow long and combing it to the side. I now understand exactly how he feels.

∞∞∞

Finding the right support group is like buying a new pair of shoes. You may have to try on a few before you find the right fit.

No More Bad-Hair Days

There are always compensations
in life. Although my hair has fallen out,
my fingernails have grown
stronger and longer.

∞∞∞

Chemotherapy is a love-hate affair.
You love that it can cure you. You hate how it
makes you feel while doing so.

There are not enough prunes in the world
to cure the kind of constipation brought on
by chemotherapy.

∞∞∞

Tears can cleanse your soul.

∞∞∞

Plant a garden — even if it is only
in one small flowerpot.

No More Bad-Hair Days

Eat whatever tastes good.
This is not the time to worry about your figure.

⚬⚬⚬⚬⚬

Telephone friends and tell them
that you love them.

⚬⚬⚬⚬⚬

During recovery, do at least one
"normal" activity each day.

Hold a baby in your arms.

∞∞∞

"That which doesn't kill you
makes you stronger."

∞∞∞

Set goals. Make plans. Just do it.

∞∞∞

Become your own favorite heroine.

No More Bad-Hair Days

I prefer quality to quantity, but I still
plan to live a long, long time.

∞∞∞

Surround yourself with happy people.

∞∞∞

Warm, chocolate-chip cookies and a cold
glass of milk have great curative powers.

Look at yourself kindly. A bald head
and a scarred body are not reflective of
who you have become.

∞∞∞∞∞

If you put on a happy face, your heart
will follow suit.

∞∞∞∞∞

Pretend that you are on summer vacation.
Read all the books you never had time for.

Vanity just sort of flies out the window
when you become a hairless wonder.

∞∞∞

Be an inspiration to your friends and family.

∞∞∞

I am spending less and less time
applying make-up because I have fewer and
fewer places to put it!

Fear is the midnight thief who
robs you of your beauty sleep.

∞∞∞

TODAY really is the first day of
the rest of your life.

∞∞∞

Select something from a mail-order
catalogue. Order it. Give yourself
something to look forward to.

Do not mistake your doctor for God.

∞∞∞

Chemotherapy is like living with a
mediocre husband; can't live with him, but
not certain that you can live without him.

∞∞∞

Rediscovering old friends is as wonderful as
opening gifts on Christmas morning.

After being on morphine for a week,
I now have a better understanding of
Timothy Leary and the '60s.

∞∞∞

Friends are like jewels; each has
a special sparkle and shine.

∞∞∞

There are no gloomy days, only gloomy people.

Smile at strangers.
You'll both feel better.

∞∞∞

Take pride in your fortitude.

∞∞∞

Big, shiny earrings and a snappy bandanna on
your head are a dazzling combination.

At least once a day, everyday, remind yourself
that you are, indeed, an amazing woman!

∞∞∞

A smile is a gift that you can
give again and again.

∞∞∞

Patience is a virtue. If not naturally
blessed with it, try to develop it.

There is a reason that the
Lord's Prayer is so popular.

∞∞∞

Don't beat yourself up over
what you should have done or might
have been. The past is past.

∞∞∞

When talking on the phone,
put a smile in your voice.

Imagine.

∞∞∞

No more bad-hair days.

∞∞∞

Recycle. Planet Earth is worth saving
whether you're on it or not.

∞∞∞

A spoonful of courage
helps the medicine go down.

No More Bad-Hair Days

It is necessary to see beyond
that which you actually can see.

∞∞∞

If you don't have the will,
you won't find the way.

∞∞∞

My friends have brought me so much
chicken soup that I expect to grow feathers
and start clucking at any moment.

Never forget how much
you have to be grateful for.

∞∞∞

Being a Southern girl, I was born batting
my eyelashes. Now I have no eyelashes.
What's a girl to do? Oh, well,
I'll think about that tomorrow.

∞∞∞

Chemotherapy causes strange side effects.
If something bizarre occurs in your body,
don't hesitate to call your doctor. He needs to
hear about the weird stuff.

Angels abound. But they usually wear
regular clothes and seldom remember to clip
on their wings or polish their halos.

∞∞∞

Return phone calls. Talking helps.

∞∞∞

Think of yourself as an Olympian — a pole
vaulter soaring toward the sun, a gymnast on
the balance beam, a kayaker negotiating rapids,
a marathoner in a race for life. You are all of
those people, and wellness is your gold medal.

No More Bad-Hair Days

We are all on the same journey with
the same destination. Take time to enjoy
the scenery along the way.

∞∞∞

There is a lot to be said
for keeping up appearances.

∞∞∞

Perfume is a lovely reminder that you are still
a lady, no matter what parts are missing.

Chocolate helps me cope.

∞∞∞

Clean out your closets and make a
charitable donation. There are many people
who are in worse shape than you.

∞∞∞

The day before you're scheduled for
chemotherapy, do something fun. It takes
your mind off what lies ahead.

Friendship is always a two-way street.

◇◇◇◇◇

Drink your juice, water, milk, etc.,
in a wine glass. You won't feel so deprived
about giving up alcohol.

◇◇◇◇◇

Even if your budget is limited,
treat yourself to little pleasures — a bouquet
of flowers, a paperback book, a Dove bar.
Remind yourself that you are special.

Attend a family reunion. You will be amazed
at how happy everyone is to see you.

∞∞∞

Really, do stop and smell the roses . . .
and the gardenias and the lilies of the field.
Pick a few, too.

∞∞∞

" . . . We will grieve not, rather find strength
in what remains behind. . . ." (Wordsworth)

No More Bad-Hair Days

Not for one moment have I missed shaving my
legs, but I always miss shampooing my hair.

∞∞∞

Act silly. Giggle. Goof-off.
Belly laugh. Be raucous. Tickle yourself with
your own good humor.

∞∞∞

Wear sexy lingerie.

Don't get pea-green with envy when
your friends get to do things that you
still can't. Your day will come.

∞∞∞

When your doctor gives you a good report,
rejoice. You may not yet have won the war,
but at least you are winning the battles.

∞∞∞

Keep a list of the books you read.
By the time you're well, you'll feel as if you've
completed a graduate degree in literature.

Movies are still the best escape, and big
screens are still better than VCRs.

∞∞∞

Buy yourself an assortment of toothbrushes,
and brush your teeth umpteen times a day.

∞∞∞

Use toothpaste that has peroxide as an
ingredient. Gargle with warm salt water.
This will help prevent mouth problems
associated with chemotherapy.

This is not morbid. This is necessary.
Write your will.

∞∞∞

Who would you really like to be
when you grow up?

∞∞∞

If you think of yourself as a cat,
you'll be amazed at how often you
land on your feet.

Continue to make plans.

∞∞∞

"Store-bought hair" and some extra make-up
can make you feel like a movie star.

∞∞∞

While waiting for appointments, be
"Chatty Cathy" talking with other patients.
It may give you a whole new outlook on life.

If your chemotherapy is an all-day event,
wear socks to keep your tootsies toasty.

∞∞∞

If you discover a natural cure for insomnia,
telephone me at once.
I'll be up waiting for your call.

∞∞∞

Eat your veggies.
(But only if they are cooked.)

No More Bad-Hair Days

Until I had cancer and had to
learn to rest, I never realized how
wonderfully decadent a lazy day can be.

∞∞∞

Ex-husbands should stay that way.

∞∞∞

This illness has taught me that there is no
time to waste. Now is absolutely the time to
tidy up your life and tie up loose ends.

We all know that old chestnut, "Fools rush in where angels fear to tread." Well, I'm no angel, and I'm certainly ready for a little foolishness.

∞∞∞

I've worn three different wigs, cotton bandannas, fancy silk scarves, and knit caps. The only thing left is to show up with a lampshade on my head.

∞∞∞

I'm ordering 10 pounds of wildflower seeds. Think of the possibilities. Wildflowers are just as tenacious as I feel. What an inspiration those flowers will be.

Continue to reinvent yourself. The new you
will be smarter, better, stronger.

∞∞∞

Think of chemotherapy as a major
renovation on your bodily home.

∞∞∞

If a little kindness goes a long way, then try a
big dose and see what the possibilities are.

Don't expect your children to
handle your illness like adults.

∞∞∞

My face broke out this week. My
dermatologist said that it was a sign that my
body was returning to normal. I never thought
that I would be so happy to see a pimple.

∞∞∞

Don't stare at yourself too long while naked.
You'll begin to feel like an alien.

Tell your nurses how much you appreciate their help. Bake them a cake or take them a box of chocolates. These ladies are helping to save your life. Let them know you've noticed.

∞∞∞

Male-female relationships are difficult enough when you're in top form. They are just about impossible when 90% of your focus is on you. Get well, and *then* get a boyfriend.

No More Bad-Hair Days

Useless song of the day: "I'm gonna
wash that man right out of my hair. . . ."

∞∞∞

Even after a complete and radical hysterectomy
— when all of your lady parts are gone —
if a handsome man smiles at you,
you still feel like a girl.

∞∞∞

Time flies whether you're having fun or not.

I managed to get through three
pregnancies with no morning sickness.
Now, with chemotherapy, I know
what I missed.

∞∞∞

Maintaining dignity while in the hospital is
next to impossible.

∞∞∞

When you are housebound, even junk
mail is something to look forward to.

∞∞∞

Faith and hope have become
my two favorite words.

Take a chance. Renew a magazine
subscription for three years instead of one.

∞∞∞

I always wear the same dress to
chemotherapy. When this ordeal is finished,
I shall have a ceremonial burning of that
dress and dance merrily around the bonfire.

No More Bad-Hair Days

Do instant-gratification household tasks.
Water droopy plants. Polish a piece of silver.
Clear out your recipe file. You'll feel an
immediate sense of accomplishment.

∞∞∞

Everyday seems like Halloween
when dealing with wigs.

∞∞∞

Each day as I grow stronger, I realize
that life offers endless possibilities.

No More Bad-Hair Days

Just for a short time, no more
"hair-raising" schemes.

∞∞∞

Chemotherapy sometimes causes
temporary, momentary amnesia. This
often works to your advantage.

∞∞∞

Learning to draw eyebrows where
there are none takes an artist's touch.

The four *R*s for cancer patients:
Resting, Relaxing, Reading, Reflection.

∞∞∞∞

Learn to listen with your ears and your heart.

∞∞∞∞

Keep a bottle of spring water in the
refrigerator. Tie a pink ribbon on it to
mark it as yours so that no one else
is tempted to sneak sips.

Depression is an unwanted visitor. Don't
let it become a permanent room-mate.

∞∞∞

If you believe that things will
get better, they will.

∞∞∞

Don't say, "*If* I get well . . ." — instead,
"*When* I get well . . ."

There is a big learning curve for cancer.

⁘

Cuddle a kitten. Purring is
one of those sweet mysteries of life.

⁘

Hot ginger tea is an excellent
tummy soother.

Question your doctor.

∞∞∞

Museums offer a respite from
everyday cares and concerns.

∞∞∞

Miracles do happen.
You can be one.

Be careful what you wish for.
I always wished for thick, coarse, wavy hair.
Now I have it — a wig!

∞∞∞

Go to a park and feed the birds.

∞∞∞

Sometimes I am shameless. If I don't want
to do something, I simply say, "Oh, I can't do
that. I have cancer." It works like a charm.

Does anyone know how to tie one of those
skimpy hospital gowns so that (1) they stay
tied and (2) your fanny doesn't hang out?

∞∞∞

This is only a chapter, not
the complete book of your life.

∞∞∞

Writing is terrific therapy. It doesn't matter
what you write, just write.

No More Bad-Hair Days

Stop worrying so much about
your future. Just be glad you have one.

∞

We all fall in love with our doctors.

∞

Sign up for a *continuing* education class.

No More Bad-Hair Days

I have scars in my neck from feeding tubes.
A scar on my chest from my port-a-cath.
Another huge scar right down my middle
from my surgery. Sometimes I feel
like the bride of Frankenstein.

∞∞∞

My definition of courage:
appearing without my wig before
my teenage son and his friends.

Spend some time seriously thinking about
all of the things you have learned since you
were first diagnosed with cancer.
Mind-boggling, isn't it?

∞∞∞

A FAVORITE OLD JOKE:

"Doctor, when I'm cured,
will I be able to tap dance?"

"Well, yes, certainly."

"Great, because I never could before."

I'm certain that there are many, many things
worse than having cancer. But I swear,
sometimes, I cannot think of a single one.

∞∞∞

Everybody who has experienced a
life-threatening illness gets depressed. You
may think that your life is over. It is not. It
has just taken a different direction.

"This is the Lord's day. Let us rejoice
and be glad in it." Now *that* is a great
thought to begin your day.

∞∞∞

There must be something that you really
want to do. What's holding you back?

∞∞∞

Intellectually, I understand that chocolate
contains no medicinal properties.
Nonetheless, whenever I eat
a brownie, I feel better.

Strive to be the person people think you are.

∞∞∞

Music definitely affects your mood.
At the moment, I'm avoiding the blues.

∞∞∞

Garrison Keillor and "Prairie Home
Companion" make mighty fine companions
on a dateless Saturday night.

Re-think your options.

∞∞∞∞

You know absolutely that you have too
much time on your hands when you begin to
ponder such questions as, "Who invented
soap-on-a-rope and why?"

∞∞∞∞

I met a lady today. A cancer survivor.
She had thick, wavy, silky hair. Hair the color
of diamonds. I instinctively reached out to
touch her hair. She smiled and said,
"Yes, it does grow back."

There is *always* a light at the end
of the tunnel. Some tunnels are just
longer than others.

∞∞∞

If you don't have a hobby, get one.

∞∞∞

After months of celibacy, I feel like
a self-rejuvenating virgin.

Go to church. Do it religiously.

∞∞∞

Even if you can't play,
you can be a cheerleader.

∞∞∞

Sometimes I feel just like a plucked chicken!

∞∞∞

When reading the newspaper,
just skip the obituaries.

It used to be that when I came home from work, the first things I took off were shoes and pantyhose. Now, it's my wig!

∞∞∞

Look forward to doing something that you've always wanted to do but have never had the nerve to try before.

∞∞∞

A flirtatious man can really lift your spirits!

Before cancer, I was a great participant
in life. During my illness, I've become an
observer of life. When I am well, I hope to
achieve a balance between the two.

∞∞∞

Don't tell me that I can't,
because I'm certain that I can.

∞∞∞

Did you ever think that you would
know more about cancer than you ever
really wanted to know?

Waiting for test results is the most
difficult part of the treatment.

∞∞∞

Wouldn't you love to "just say no" to drugs?

∞∞∞

Friends have given me so many good-
luck charms that I'm starting to feel like
a voodoo high priestess.

The longer you are without hair, the less self-conscious you will become. Like anything else, it just takes getting used to.

∞∞∞

There is infinite goodness in the world.

∞∞∞

My mother used to say, "True friends are like diamonds, precious and rare." She was, as always, right.

My energy usually evaporates by 4:00 P.M. Consequently, I now plan my social outings as daytime events. Meeting friends for lunch is just as much fun as meeting for dinner — and it is less expensive.

∞∞∞

When getting dressed, always put your wig on at the last possible minute; for the longer you wear it, the more uncomfortable it gets.

∞∞∞

Life is too short to date (or be married to) a man who doesn't appreciate you.

The less you complain,
the better you will feel.

∞∞∞

Keep a paperback book in your purse.
Frequently, there is absolutely nothing to
read in the waiting room.

∞∞∞

Cancer is a humbling experience, but you
still have every right to be proud of yourself.

No More Bad-Hair Days

Perrier poured into a flute bubbles
just like champagne. Pretend!

∞∞∞

Frequently your nurses will have more
answers than your doctors.

∞∞∞

Never try to balance your checkbook
when you are taking pain pills!

As your body gets weaker,
force your mind to grow stronger.

∞∞

There are many types of
chemotherapy. There are countless
side-effects from it. But the universal
reaction to chemotherapy is *dread*.

∞∞

Don't ever start any thought with
"I'm dying to . . ."

82

Many of my friends are dealing with
various illnesses. We discuss our surgeries,
our scars, our treatments. None of it
seems so awful when shared.

∞∞∞

Each night before I go to bed, I refill my
bird feeder. The early birds get sunflower
seeds instead of worms. And I have a
feast for my eyes, as bright and beautiful
birds fly about my yard.

No More Bad-Hair Days

We don't say "battling cancer"
without good reason.

∞∞∞

There are no bad vintages for cranberry juice
— always light and fruity with luscious color.
Just think of it as a very nouveau Beaujolais!

∞∞∞

While undergoing chemotherapy, I'm positive
that I've never, not once, experienced a single
coherent thought. My brain leaves my body.

Cancer is not contagious. However,
the way some people react to it, you
would think that it is.

∞∞∞

Do not think of yourself as a "victim."

∞∞∞

Treat your illness like a job, and
work diligently at getting well.

If your friends are kind enough to run
errands for you, let them. Save what energy
you have for the "fun stuff."

∞∞∞

I don't know why bad things happen
to good people. Maybe it's a reminder that
none of us is as good as we think, and,
perhaps, could be better.

∞∞∞

Though I've not undergone radiation therapy,
chemotherapy gives me a bright pink, rosy
glow. I look as though I've been nuked.

A-tisket, a-tasket. Buy yourself a basket —
one with dividers. In it keep stationery, pens,
scissors, a small stapler, extra reading glasses,
stamps, your address book with pertinent
phone numbers, paper clips. Keep the basket
within easy reach. You'll be amazed at how
often you need these items and how much
energy you'll save by not scurrying
around looking for them.

Psychologically, preparing for chemotherapy is
just like bracing for a hurricane. You know that
the storm will hit, you just don't know when.

∞∞∞

Sometimes I feel as if I'm running on empty,
but at least I'm still running.

∞∞∞

During your illness you will be surprised
by the friends who stand by you and those
who disappear. Cancer is a reminder of our
mortality. Not everyone can face that.

Wearing wigs can feel just like
playing "dress-up."

∞∞∞

I stay tired. But amazingly I can
muster the energy to do what appeals
to me. Mind over matter.

∞∞∞

It's not true that you can never be "too rich
or too thin." The "too rich" part is true, but
"too thin" is detrimental to wellness.

You have to bloom sometime.

∞∞∞

All cancer scars are not visible.

∞∞∞

Visit with small children. They are
filled with wisdom and wonder.

∞∞∞

Just let the universe take over. It's a
new-age kind of thing, but it seems to work.

Read books that you ordinarily wouldn't.
It will open your mind and start new
thought processes.

∞∞∞

While you are unable to work,
just think of the money you are saving
on dry-cleaning bills!

∞∞∞

Learn all that you possibly can from
your experience. Share your knowledge.
You may help save a life!

Even a broken heart can be full.

∞∞∞

Keep a book of favorite poetry close at hand.
Beautiful poems can instantly transport your
thoughts to a better place.

∞∞∞

There is a lot to be said for not having to
wear pantyhose everyday!

The paradox of illness is this: It can make
you grow up fast, but you'll still long to
do simple, childish things.

∞∞∞

There are times when I think about
cancer and absolutely nothing
humorous comes to mind.

∞∞∞

As sick as you are, you'll still have to
constantly remind your teenager to
take out the garbage.

If full growth takes many years,
I hope the Lord is paying attention.

∞∞∞

Don't second-guess decisions that
you made concerning your cancer.
You can make yourself nuts thinking
"What if . . . ?"

∞∞∞

I understand that having a life-threatening
disease builds character. I didn't need the
disease. I already was one.

My razor, unused and rusty, is still in
my shower. It serves as a daily reminder that
one day life will return to normal, and
I will again have to shave.

∞∞∞

Your relationship with your chemotherapy
nurse often feels like a bad marriage —
you just want it to end.

I used to say, "I laughed myself to death."
Now I prefer, "I laughed so hard I cried." Just
avoid the *d* word whenever possible.

∞∞∞

All of those fat cells that disappeared
when you were sick and skinny will
miraculously find their way back as
your health and appetite improve.
Cellulite shows no mercy.

When you're not wearing your wig,
put it away. Don't toss it down casually
because it will look like a small, dead
animal. Not a pretty sight.

∞∞

I look at my big scar differently now and
view it as "The Red Badge of Courage."

∞∞

I have collected so many hats that
my next career could be as a
second-hand haberdasher.

Today is my last chemotherapy treatment!
Strange that you can look forward
to something so awful!

∞∞∞

Did you ever think that you would miss
something so tedious as plucking
your eyebrows?

∞∞∞

Standing very straight and tall, I am 5'3".
Having survived cancer and chemotherapy,
I often feel like Superwoman.

There will be days when you feel as if
you are donating your body to science. You are.

∞∞∞

At some point, you will be given a schedule
and a number of expected chemotherapy
treatments. Don't count on it! The dictates
of cancer can change everything.

∞∞∞

I now have great admiration and
respect for guinea pigs.

No More Bad-Hair Days

Holding grudges only hurts you.

∞∞∞∞

THINGS THAT YOU PROBABLY WON'T NEED
THROUGHOUT YOUR CHEMOTHERAPY:
mascara, eyelash curler, hot rollers,
hair spray, haircuts
WHAT YOU NEED INSTEAD:
faith, hope, love, patience,
a sense of humor

It is not true that you can't teach an
old dog new tricks. I am learning something
new about myself every day.

∞∞∞

The best advice you can receive is to
make the most of each day. We are never
promised tomorrow.

∞∞∞

Be open to alternative theories.
You don't have to be Chinese to benefit
from acupuncture.

Learn to meditate.

∞∞∞∞

Fake it 'til you make it!

∞∞∞∞

No matter what anyone says,
for a woman who is used to having hair,
BALD is not sexy!

A wonderful and very supportive friend told
me that there are only two definites in life:
(1) We take a first breath, and
(2) we take a final breath. Everything else
is unwritten in our life-script.

∞∞∞

Southern Bell said it best:
"Reach out and touch someone."

Negatives can turn into positives in the blink
of an eye. My dog ran away, and the nice lady
who brought him home has become a new
and positive force in my life.

ooooo

If your illness reaches a point where medical
science can no longer help, and your doctor
says that your days are numbered, treat this
information like a precious gift. There are
truly no moments to waste.

Deep within us all, there is a well-spring of
courage that bubbles up and provides us with
the hope that we will be well again.

∞∞∞

I would hate to leave
before the party is over.

Acknowledgments

Thank you to my guardian angels who appeared as if
by magic to cook, clean, chaffeur, comfort:

ooooo

Alyson Orr
Davalyn Palmer
Fay Mann
Joanne Ackerman
Suzie Holly
Vi Hill
Mary Beth and Steve Whitmire
Penny Schwab
Judy Foster
Carol Bosworth
Jean Thornton
Sheila Lichtman
Mimi Wilson
Janet and Whit Hagerman
Jacqueline Couch
Ruby Smith
Francis Bee
Norman Zapien
Mary Courim
Ann Dickey
Dotti Nacci

Claudia, Anne, and Sheryl
Frank C.
Bill Bishop
Dan and Deborah Benardot
Dominique Chambon
Madeline Guadagnino
Arlene Miller
Robin Rodbel
Diane and Tom Casey
Kathy Roberts
Leslie Greenberg

My friends at
"Where-Atlanta," William's
Salon, and Saint Dunstan's and
my children: Susanna, Nicholas,
and Vanessa

Special thanks to Melissa Libby
who first suggested these thoughts
should be a book